WELCOME TO THE WORLD OF
Wild Horses

Diane Swanson

Whitecap Books

Edited by Elizabeth McLean
Cover design by Steve Penner
Interior design by Margaret Ng
Typeset by Jacqui Thomas
Photo research by Tanya Lloyd Kyi
Cover photograph by Darrell Gulin/Dembinsky Photo Assoc
Photo credits: Darrell Gulin/Dembinsky Photo Assoc iv, 10, 20; Lynn M. Stone 2, 8, 18, 22, 24; Dominique Braud/Dembinsky Photo Assoc 4, 12, 14, 26; Paul Rezendes 6; David A. Ponton/www.firstlight.ca 16

Printed and bound in Canada

National Library of Canada Cataloguing in Publication Data

Swanson, Diane, 1944–
    Welcome to the world of wild horses

    Includes index.
    ISBN 1-55285-321-7 (bound).—ISBN 1-55285-320-9 (pbk.)

    1. Wild Horses—North America—Juvenile literature. I. Title.
QL737.U62S92 2002   j599.665′5′097   C2002-910081-X

For more information on this series and other Whitecap Books titles, visit our web site at www.whitecap.ca

The publisher acknowledges the support of the Canada Council for the Arts and the Cultural Services Branch of the Government of British Columbia for our publishing program. We acknowledge the financial support of the Government of Canada through the Book Publishing Industry Development Program for our publishing activities.

Contents

World of Difference

WITH HOOVES POUNDING AND TAILS FLYING, wild horses gallop across fields and meadows. They look as if they've always run free, but few have. The only truly wild horses in the world today are the little Przewalski's (psha-VAL-skeez) horses of Mongolia. The rest are called "feral," meaning they live wild now, but their families didn't start off that way.

Thousands of years ago, horses died out in North America. But before they did, some of them traveled across a land bridge to Asia, then on to Europe and Africa. Many were tamed to help people.

Off and running! A wild horse races with the wind.

1

This young foal
is taking life easy,
snatching a nap on
the soft grass.

Most of the wild horses in North
America now descended from tame animals
that arrived with Spanish explorers about
500 years ago. Some came later with settlers
from other countries, such as France.

A number of these horses escaped or
were abandoned, but they learned to survive.
They managed to struggle through severe

weather, adapt to new homes, and find enough food to eat. Over time, their hard lives made the horses tougher. They mated with one another, and their young, called foals, were born wild.

Zebras and asses are the closest relatives of horses. The differences among them are few. Zebras are striped all over, while asses have longer ears. Horses are usually taller. Many stand more than 1.5 metres (5 feet) high at the shoulder. Short horses are sometimes called ponies.

Wild horses didn't always look like they do now. About 60 million years ago, their early ancestors—called dawn horses—were only the size of large hares. Their back feet had three toes and their front feet had four.

Over time, horses grew bigger and their legs became longer. Their toes decreased in number but increased in size. Today, each foot has one broad toe with a thick claw—a hoof— that helps the horses speed across grasslands.

Where in the World

MOST CONTINENTS ARE HOME TO WILD, OR FERAL, HORSES. In North America, they live mainly in the West. Some have settled on small islands off the Atlantic coast.

Wild horses often gather on open stretches of land. They can survive on rugged grasslands where little rain falls or on sandy islands. Day to day, they're on the move, searching for new or better feeding spots.

Unlike tame horses on ranches or farms, wild horses can have trouble finding shelter from extreme weather. They may gather in canyons to try to escape cold blasts of wind.

A band of wild horses searches for food in the American West.

5

Wild horses struggle to survive on Assateague Island on the edge of the Atlantic.

And before wintertime, they may grow longer, shaggy hair that helps keep them warm.

In some places, governments have set aside land for wild horses. On the Pryor Mountain Wild Horse Range of Montana, for instance, the horses don't have to compete with tame animals, such as cattle and sheep, for food.

Wherever they're found, wild horses form family groups. These bands are usually made up of several females, called mares, and their young, or foals. Each band is headed by a male, called a stallion, that is six or more years old. One of the mares may lead the horses to food, water, and shelter. The stallion follows behind, where he can protect the band from enemies such as wolves.

Wild horses aren't nearly as common today as they once were. There is far less room for them to roam freely.

NEW HOMES FOR HORSES

Small wild horses, also called ponies, live on Assateague Island of Virginia and Maryland. Legends say they once survived a shipwreck, or they were abandoned by farmers. The horses feed on coarse marsh grasses—even on moss and poison ivy.

To keep some of the bands from getting too crowded, volunteer firefighters hold a yearly auction. Horses are made to swim to nearby Chincoteague Island, where people buy them to tame for riding. And the money supports firefighting.

7

World Full of Food

EATING TAKES MOST OF THE DAY— for a wild horse. It needs 11 to 14 kilograms (24 to 30 pounds) of food every 24 hours. That's not too hard to find during the summer when a horse can munch on grass and the leaves from shrubs. But in winter, a wild horse depends more on twigs and plant roots, which it digs up with its hooves. Near the ocean, it might add a little seaweed to its meals.

Depending on where they live, some wild horses have to work harder than others to get food. They might have to paw through sand dunes or snowdrifts—even

Snip, snip. Wild horses spend much of their time grazing.

9

Wading into
a pond, thirsty
horses stop
for a drink.

crack the frozen sea spray that coats grass along cold shores.

Finding enough food to fill all the members of a band can be tough. Wild horses not only compete with one another for meals, but also with other grazers, including elk, pronghorn antelopes, and rabbits.

Given all the time a horse spends eating,

it's lucky it is so well equipped for the job. A long flexible neck helps it reach the ground while the horse is standing. Sharp front teeth can easily slice off big mouthfuls of grass. And thick, ridged cheek teeth stand up to the wear and tear of chewing tough food thoroughly.

A horse's eyes are also specially designed for mealtimes. They can focus on close objects below eye level, such as grass, while also watching for objects higher up and farther away—such as hungry mountain lions.

QUENCHING THAT THIRST

Wild horses don't need a lot of water. They usually drink just once or twice a day. Where the land is very dry, the horses may stay within about 5 kilometres (3 miles) of a pond or river. Then they can be sure to have a drink when they need one.

Whenever water is scarce, wild horses might only drink every second day. They may have to break through ice or dig through soil to find hidden water.

World of Words

FAMILY MEMBERS TALK WITH ONE ANOTHER—and wild horses are no exception. They use sound, body language, or both to get their messages across. For instance, if one of the mares in a band strays too far, the stallion tells her to return by arching his neck and shaking his head.

The stallion always stands guard for his band, frequently poking his nose in the air to check for the scent of enemies. If he sniffs danger, he immediately warns the others. Snorting madly, he races—head down—toward the band. The message is clear: "Get away from here!"

A horse raises and lowers its ears to "talk" to others.

A horse can say, "I'm mad," with its ears. It flattens them and points them back on its head. If the horse is feeling aggressive, it might also open its mouth, drawing up the corners to show its many large teeth.

A display of teeth can be a friendly greeting, too, but the horse wouldn't draw up the

Curling his lip, a stallion picks up a scent message: a mare is ready to mate.

corners of its mouth. And it would stand its ears straight up. It might also nibble the skin near the base of another horse's tail as a way of making the greeting warmer.

If a young male horse wants to avoid a fight with a stallion, it hangs its head low and flattens its ears, holding them sideways. That says, "You're the boss."

Like human families, bands sometimes scold their young for misbehaving. An occasional nip, even a light kick, is horse talk for "Be good!"

To a stallion, there's no such thing as plain horse manure. It's an important message that reminds others who's the boss of a band.

When a stallion discovers a pile of manure, he checks it out by sniffing. If he decides the pile was left by another stallion—or two or three others—he adds to it. Laying his scent on top is important to any stallion trying to hold onto his rank. And that beats fighting for it.

New World

COOL NIGHTS OR EARLY DAWNS. That's when wild horses are born in the spring. Mares usually don't mate with their stallion every year, and they normally have only one foal each.

As soon as a mare is ready to give birth, she leaves her band. She doesn't go far, but she finds a quiet, comfortable spot to receive her foal. She licks it gently and lets it feed on the warm milk from her body. Then she rejoins the family, bringing the newborn with her. The stallion may meet them along the way, quietly prodding them both to head back to the band.

This wild foal has no trouble finding a nutritious meal of milk.

17

It's surprising how quickly a newborn horse learns to walk—and run.

Unlike people, foals can stand and walk when they are less than an hour old. Their long, knobby legs are shaky at first. The foals stumble and teeter from side to side. They fall down, but their mothers nuzzle them, urging them to get up and try walking again.

Within a few days, the foals gain

enough strength to run—and run well. If they must, they can keep up with the other horses in their band. That's especially important if an enemy happens to be lurking nearby and the stallion urges the band to escape.

Being part of a band protects the foals in other ways, too. For example, when the weather is stormy, all the horses huddle tightly together. They turn their back ends to chilling winds and heavy rains.

Foals born on sandy Sable Island off Canada's east coast can thank children for their home. Hardy wild horses have struggled to survive there for over 250 years. But in the late 1950s, some people wanted them removed—even used for dog food.

Many children wrote letters to Canada's prime minister, begging him to let the horses be "as free as the wind." Since 1960, Canada has allowed the Sable Island bands to live as they will.

Changing World

WILD HORSES DON'T STAY WITH THEIR BANDS FOREVER. Young females might wander away on their own and enter other bands. Or they might be chased out by the mares.

A stallion keeps a watchful eye on the young males in his band. When they're two or three years old, he drives them off by acting tough. He presses his ears back flat and exposes a mouthful of teeth. He lowers his head and swings it madly from side to side. Then he lunges at the young horses, nipping them over and over. Each time, he bites a little harder, scaring them out of the band.

Sooner or later, most wild horses leave their parents and join other bands.

21

When a young stallion starts biting, the battle becomes more serious.

The young horses usually join other males of their age, forming a band with one of them as leader. They travel and eat together until they're old enough to start their own families.

At about age six, a young stallion might challenge an older one for control of a band or some of the mares. There's a lot of bluffing involved. The two males sniff and snort. With curved necks, they prance around, then stomp their hooves and paw the ground. The younger horse might give up unless he senses the older one is weaker. Then the young male would rise up on his back legs and lash out with his sharp front hooves. If that wasn't enough, he would start biting, especially on the neck and front legs.

When an old horse loses his band—and survives—he may live all alone. He'll likely reach at least age 20.

Wild horses are wonderful. Here are just a few of the reasons why:

- A horse doesn't have to lie down to rest. It can also sleep standing up.
- To scratch any hard-to-reach itches, a horse can use a stick clutched tightly between its teeth.
- The jaws of a horse are strong enough to crush the backbone of a coyote.
- A wild horse is so speedy it can outrun most of its enemies.

Fun World

HORSEPLAY MEANS ROUGH, ROWDY FUN. And that's what wild horses seem to like best.

Of all the members of a band, young foals spend the most time playing, often on their own. They leap around, kicking up their heels and twisting their long-legged bodies in midair.

When two or more foals play together, they snicker, squeal, squeak, and snort. They prance about, then zoom off, racing across an open field. Although there's nothing on their backs, they may buck crazily as if they're trying to shake something off.

Play-fighting helps foals have fun and prepares them for real fights.

25

Two wild foals
are grooming
each other.
Mmm, feels great!

Excitement can trigger horseplay.
Another horse or a rabbit bolting past can
set a foal off. Even a quiet change, such as
sunshine suddenly bursting through a cloud,
can start a foal bucking and pawing the air.
But now and then, it seems to play just
because it's feeling good.

Playing helps wild horses build strong

muscles and bones. It also helps them practice important skills. Two females might kick at each other with their back hooves without touching. It's their way of having fun and learning to protect themselves from their enemies.

Young males play as if they're fighting. They even look vicious—trying to bite each other on the face or front legs. All this horsing around will help them compete for mares one day when they're old enough to win and take charge of their own bands.

GROOMING IS GREAT

Just like playing, grooming is something horses seem to enjoy. It's good for them, too. Bathing in water or mud helps cool off their bodies, and it gets rid of some of the pests that bite them. So does rolling around on the dirt and grass or rubbing against rocks and trees.

Horses also groom one another. Using their teeth, they nibble dead skin or loose hair on their necks and backs—sometimes untangling mats. And the grooming says, "I like you."

Index

Collect all Welcome to the World titles

- [ ] **1** Welcome to the World of Wolves
- [ ] **2** Welcome to the World of Whales
- [ ] **3** Welcome to the World of Bears
- [ ] **4** Welcome to the World of Otters
- [ ] **5** Welcome to the World of Owls
- [ ] **6** Welcome to the World of Wild Cats
- [ ] **7** Welcome to the World of Eagles
- [ ] **8** Welcome to the World of Foxes
- [ ] **9** Welcome to the World of Bats
- [ ] **10** Welcome to the World of Raccoons
- [ ] **11** Welcome to the World of Beavers
- [ ] **12** Welcome to the World of Moose
- [ ] **13** Welcome to the World of Skunks
- [ ] **14** Welcome to the World of Porcupines
- [ ] **15** Welcome to the World of Octopuses
- [ ] **16** Welcome to the World of Rabbits and Hares
- [ ] **17** Welcome to the World of Sharks
- [ ] **18** Welcome to the World of Snakes
- [ ] **19** Welcome to the World of Squirrels
- [ ] **20** Welcome to the World of Coyotes
- [ ] **21** Welcome to the World of Wild Horses
- [ ] **22** Welcome to the World of Hummingbirds